15 ART SONGS BY BRITISH COMPOSERS

SONGS BY
BRITTEN, CLARKE, FINZI,
GURNEY, PURCELL, QUILTER,
VAUGHAN WILLIAMS, AND WARLOCK

To access companion recorded accompaniment online, visit:
www.halleonard.com/mylibrary

"Enter Code"
7485-4177-4409-9078

ISBN 978-1-4584-1048-1

DISTRIBUTED BY

www.boosey.com
www.halleonard.com

Contact us:
Hal Leonard
7777 West Bluemound Road
Milwaukee, WI 53213
Email: info@halleonard.com

In Europe, contact:
Hal Leonard Europe Limited
42 Wigmore Street
Marylebone, London, W1U 2RN
Email: info@halleonardeurope.com

In Australia, contact:
Hal Leonard Australia Pty. Ltd.
4 Lentara Court
Cheltenham, Victoria, 3192 Australia
Email: info@halleonard.com.au

CONTENTS

Pianists on the recordings: Richard Walters[1], Laura Ward[2]

The price of this publication includes access to companion
recorded accompaniments online, for download or streaming,
using the unique code found on the title page.
Visit **www.halleonard.com** and enter the access code.

Come you not from Newcastle?

Hullah's Song Book (English)

from *Folksong Arrangements Volume 3: British Isles*

original key: F Major

Arranged by
BENJAMIN BRITTEN

should I not speed af - ter him, since love to all is free?

Come you not from New - cas - tle?

Come you not there a - way? O met you not my

true love, rid - ing on a bon - ny bay?

Why _ should _ I ___ not love my love? ___ Why

should not my love ___ love ___ me? ___ Why _

should _ I ___ not speed af - ter him, _____ since love to

express.

all is free? _____

(in time)

Nocturne

from *On This Island*

original key: C♯ minor

W.H. AUDEN

BENJAMIN BRITTEN

horse   Or re - volt - ing suc - cu - bus;

Calm - ly till the morn - ing break__ Let him lie,

then__

gen - tly wake.__

May 5, 1937

The Nurse's Song

from *A Charm of Lullabies*

original key

JOHN PHILIP

BENJAMIN BRITTEN

In accompaniment recording, the first vocal note is played two times before the entrance.

this to de - sire ___ I will not de - lay me. This to de - sire ___ I
will not de - lay me.
più dim.

Lull - a - by - ba - by lull - a - by - la - by ba - by, Thy nurse will tend thee as
du - ly as may be. Lull - a - by - la - by - la - by - la - by ba - by.

[Dec. 1947-Aldeburgh]

For Ralph Vaughan Williams on his birthday, Oct. 12th, 1942

Come away, come away, death

from *Let Us Garlands Bring,* Op. 18

original key

WILLIAM SHAKESPEARE

GERALD FINZI

Oh fair to see

from *Oh fair to see*
original key: a minor 3rd higher

CHRISTINA ROSSETTI

GERALD FINZI

Oh fair to see
Fruit - la - den cher - ry tree, With balls of shin - ing red Deck - ing a leaf - y head; Oh fair ___ to see! ___

To Emmy Hunt
Sleep
from *Five Elizabethan Songs*
original key: B♭ minor

JOHN FLETCHER

IVOR GURNEY

Though but a shad - ow, but a slid - ing, Let me

know some lit - tle joy! _____ We that suf - fer long an - noy Are con-

colla voce

ten - ted with a thought Through an i - dle fan - cy wrought:

poco cresc.

poco cresc.

O let my joys have some a - bid - ing! _____ O let my

joys have _____ some a - bid - ing! _____

Down by the salley gardens

original key: E minor

W.B. YEATS

REBECCA CLARKE

Flowingly, in folk-song style

In accompaniment recording, the first vocal note is played two times before the entrance.

I attempt from love's sickness to fly

original key: A Major

JOHN DRYDEN
and ROBERT HOWARD

HENRY PURCELL
realized by
BENJAMIN BRITTEN

With gentle movement

For love has more pow'r and less mer - cy than fate, To make us seek

ru - in, to make us seek ru - in and love those that hate. I at-

tempt from love's sick - ness to fly in vain, Since

I am my - self my own fe - ver, since I am my - self my own fe - ver and pain.

If music be the food of love
(1st Version)
original key: G minor

HENRY HEVENINGHAM

HENRY PURCELL
realized by
BENJAMIN BRITTEN

In accompaniment recording, the first chord is played before the entrance.

To Mrs. E.P. Balmain

Now sleeps the crimson petal

from Three Songs, Op. 3

original key: E-flat Major

ALFRED TENNYSON

ROGER QUILTER

Now sleeps the crim - son pe - tal, now the white;

Nor waves the cy - press in the pa - lace walk;

Nor winks the gold fin in the porph' - ry font: The

fire - fly wa - kens: wa - ken thou with me.

con passione

Now folds the li - ly all her sweet - ness up,

And slips in-to the bo-som of the lake;

So fold thy-self, my dear-est, thou, and slip,

In-to my bo-som and be lost, be

lost in me.

To Gervase Elwes

Love's Philosophy

from Three Songs, Op. 3

original key: F Major

PERCY B. SHELLEY

ROGER QUILTER

40

To the memory of my friend, Mrs. Cary-Elwes

Weep you no more

from *Seven Elizabethan Lyrics*

original key: F minor

ANONYMOUS

ROGER QUILTER

To Mrs. Edmund Fisher

Linden Lea
A Dorset Song
original key

WILLIAM BARNES

RALPH VAUGHAN WILLIAMS

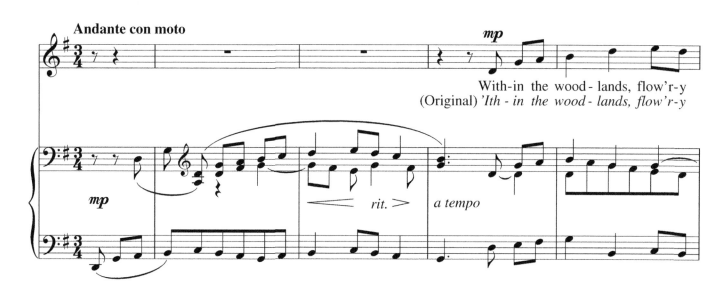

With-in the wood - lands, flow'r-y
(Original) *'Ith - in the wood - lands, flow'r-y*

glad - ed, By the oak trees' moss - y moot; The shin-ing grass blades, tim-ber shad - ed, Now do
glëad - ed, By the woak trees' moss - y moot, The sheen-en grass blëades, tim-ber shëad - ed, Now do

quiv-er un - der foot; And birds do whis - tle o - ver-head, And wa-ter's bub - bling in its
quiv-er un - der voot; An' birds do whis - sle au-ver-head, An' wa-ter's bub - blen in its

bed;   And there for me,   The ap-ple tree Do lean down low in Lin-den Lea

bed;   An' there vor me,   The ap-ple tree Do lean down low in Lin-den Lea.

When leaves, that late - ly   were a-spring-ing, Now do

When leaves, that lëate - ly   were a-spring-en, Now do

fade with-in   the   copse,   And paint-ed birds   do   hush their sing - ing, Up up-

fade 'ith-in   the   copse,   An' paint-ed birds   do   hush their zing - en, Up up-

master, Though no man may heed my frowns. I be free to go a-
meäs - ter, Though noo man may heed my frowns. I be free to go a-

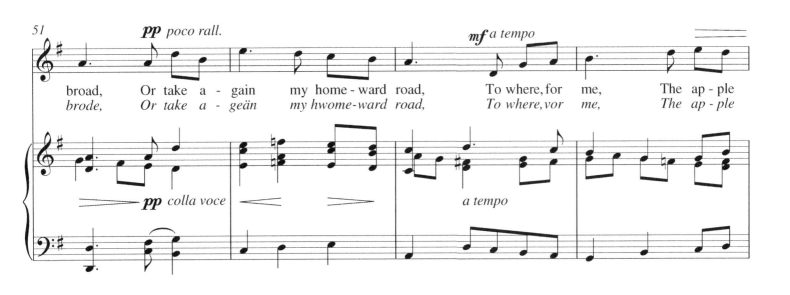

broad, Or take a - gain my home - ward road, To where, for me, The ap - ple
brode, Or take a - geän my hwome-ward road, To where, vor me, The ap - ple

tree Do lean down low in Lin - den Lea.
tree Do lean down low in Lin - den Lea.

The Vagabond

from *Songs of Travel*

original key

R. L. STEVENSON

RALPH VAUGHAN WILLIAMS

Allegro moderato
(Alla marcia)

Give to me the life I love, Let the lave go

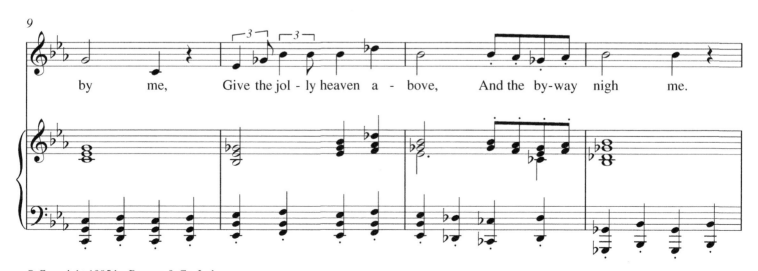

by me, Give the jol - ly heaven a - bove, And the by-way nigh me.

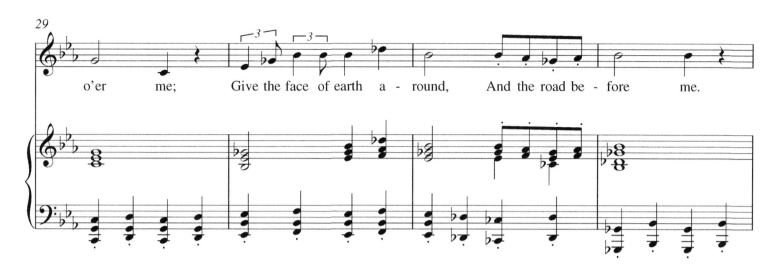

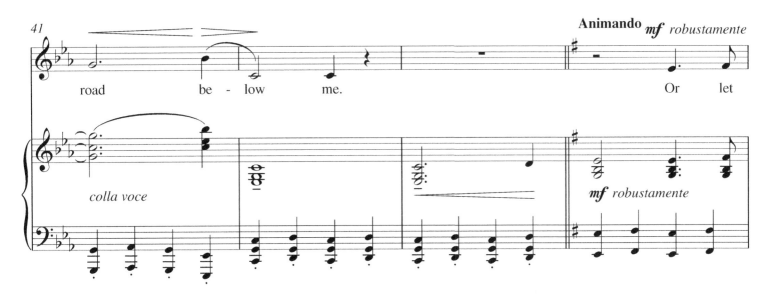

Take, O take those lips away

original key: F♯ minor

WILLIAM SHAKESPEARE

PETER WARLOCK

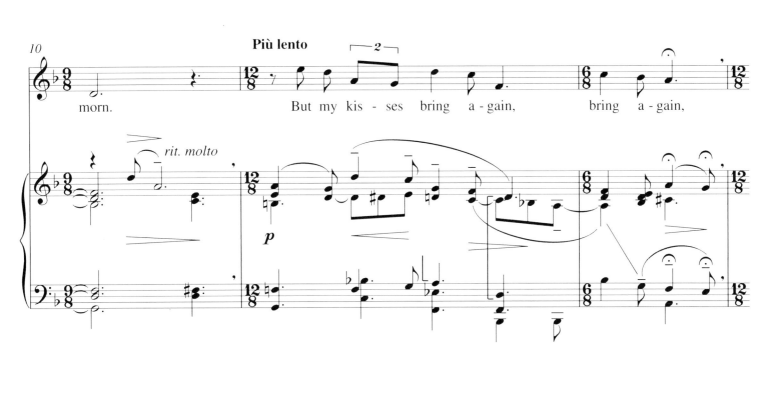

Più lento

morn. But my kis - ses bring a - gain, bring a - gain,

Seals of love, but seal'd _____ in vain, seal'd in vain! _____

dim. p mf ritenuto

dim.

p pp ppp

Ped. al fine